HOW TO WIN ARGUMENTS AND P**S PEOPLE OFF

YOU DON'T HAVE TO BE SMARTER TO BE RIGHT. USE CREATIVE, CRITICAL THINKING. REFRAME WITH LOGIC AND HUMOR.

JORDAN ELLIOTT

CONTENTS

INTRODUCTION

Hello there, how are you doing? Y'all good? I hope so, and I hope you're even better by the end of this book! That's the aim; the intent; the purpose for my writing it. But enough about me, tell me about you. What are your aims or intent? What is your purpose for reading this book? A little hard to give me an answer through the page, I know. So, just think it over for me, and as you read the chapters to follow, keep it in mind.

In the following pages, we're going to cover a number of tools and techniques from the world of neuro-linguistic programming (NLP) that will not only help you in the art of conversation and persuasion, but in every aspect of your life. By the end, you'll know everything you need to start winning every argument and knowing how to piss people off the right way. Let's face it, you're not going to get very far in life without pissing off at least a few people along the way. This is even more true when it comes to trying to change people's beliefs or alter their way of thinking to better reflect your argument points or point of view. Since this is one of the central aims of this book, and it's an inevitability attached to it, we may as well learn how to piss people off with panache.

Get ready for a journey through the world of conversation, argumentation, reframing, and persuasion as we learn about neuro-linguistic programming (NLP) and how to use it to become the conversation king or persuasion queen of your wildest dreams. As we shall see, the ability to be a wizard with words, or to be the context-setter of every conversation, isn't something that you either have or you don't; it's something that you learn. That something is exactly what I'm here to teach you about today. So, thanks for coming! Turn the page and let's begin.

1

THE GRASS IS GREEN AND THE SKY IS BLUE, ISN'T IT?

Hard fact: You can't get anywhere substantial in life without pissing a few people off along the way, and if you thought you could, sorry not sorry. At least you've picked up this book so I can show you how to piss people off the right way. By the end, you'll be able to break down and take apart any person's argument; dividing, conquering, and destroying them so that you get what you want.

Seems a bit harsh, I know, but with practice and the techniques we'll cover in this book, it won't seem like you are attacking someone or forcing your views on others. Rather, people will start to think of you as some kind of magician; a wizard with words who can successfully challenge what seemed to everyone else as being a cold, hard fact. Before you countered and proved them wrong, that is.

Is the grass really green and the sky really blue? Believe it or not, one can very logically oppose even these proverbial "truths". Just make sure to do so in a way that pisses people off in the right way. It can be very off-putting for those that are the target of your argumentative prowess. As such, it's important to learn how to read the signs that you are irritating those that oppose you in the wrong way. In other words, we need to learn how to piss people in a way that makes them love us all the more for it.

In this chapter, we'll begin by chatting about how to piss people the right way, going over the basics of how to correctly express yourself and assert your authority before diving into the benefits of pissing people off. Let's begin our journey into the world of Neuro-Linguistic Programming (NLP) and learn how to use creative and critical thinking, logic, and humor to win any argument. Remember: You don't have to be smarter to be right.

THERE'S A RIGHT WAY TO PISS PEOPLE OFF

Have you ever found yourself so worried about saying something that could possibly piss someone off that you have kept your thoughts and feelings bottled up? Or, worse, have you given in to the ridiculous reasoning of another because you have been too afraid of rocking the boat? Well, that's all about to change. Believe it or not, people will respect you a whole lot more if you stand up for what you believe in and air your thoughts and opinions no matter who may try to disagree with you.

Rather than being a doormat walked over in every argument, this book will help you to set in place the solid foundations necessary to develop the fortitude of logic and reasoning that sees you outmaneuver even the most argumentative of your friends and family members. The hidden secret of those that get what they want out of a conversation is that it's less about not pissing people off and more about learning how to piss people off the right way.

If we want to leave a lasting impression on those around us or leave the world a better place than we found it, we need to speak our truth. We need to spread awareness of our passion or personal cause as far and wide as we can. If we're continuously worrying about pissing people off along the way, we won't get half as far as we could have. People tend to lash out when their world views are challenged in even the most miniscule way. This means that you could be saying something completely reasonable, but because the person you're speaking to doesn't agree with you, you piss them off. They get angry and let you know it. Other times, people are just itching for a fight and waiting for any opportunity to jump down someone, anyone's throat.

The bottom line is that their responses have nothing to do with you. It's on them. Everyone is dealing with their own demons in life, and it's not up to us to control the way they respond to what we say. Coming to terms with this is the first step to winning each and every argument you enter. It also forms the foundation of learning how to piss people off the right way.

It's All About Communication

While we don't have control over the way that others think, act, and respond to what we say, we do have control over our own thoughts, actions, and responses. We can control the way we present ourselves to the world. This will, in turn, control the way the world presents itself to us. Want to get whatever you want served to you on a golden platter? Act like you deserve nothing less. Want to win arguments and piss people off the right way? Then start acting like it!

There is a little more to it than that, as we'll get to in the chapters to follow. In this section, we'll set in place some solid foundations as we cover the communication skills necessary to begin presenting yourself in the right way. Remember that this doesn't mean hiding your true feelings from people or becoming an emotionless zombie. Emotions, like worry, frustration, or anger, can help to emphasize your point and inspire your audience to take action. Rather than donning a mask, embody your points, expressing yourself clearly, assertively, and with a pinch of panache. Let's go through the main tips and techniques you can use to up your communication game straight away!

Speak Clearly, Act Assertively

As we mentioned above, to begin pissing people off the right way, you first need to learn to communicate in a clear, assertive manner. This will make you seem like an expert or authority on any subject. Being assertive doesn't mean you have to be aggressive or combative, but rather that you speak in a straight-shooting, no-nonsense way wherein you say what you mean and expect to get what you want. Assertiveness allows you to speak about positive or negative topics without being hurtful or letting people treat you like a doormat.

To develop your assertive communication skills, begin by being an active listener. This means that you need to actively *listen* to those that you speak to, rather than just thinking of what you are going to say next. Believe it or not, thinking of what they're going to say next is what many people unskilled in the arts of communication do in a conversation. This pisses people off in the wrong way. It makes them feel like you don't care about what they have to say; like they're some kind of soundboard rather than a thinking, feeling human. Linked to active listening, developing an assertive communication style also requires a sense of personal responsibility within any conversation, respect toward your fellow people, and honesty. Finally, assertiveness also requires an understanding of compromise and how to play the fine line between being assertive and being rude or obstinate.

Get Rid of Assumptions

I'm sure that you've heard of the saying: 'To assume makes an ass out of you and me." If you haven't, well, now you know. Another quote about assumptions comes from the philosopher Eugene Lewis Fordsworthe, who said: "Assumption is the mother of all mistakes." According to Fordsworthe, assumptions are only useful when you don't have enough information about something. If this is the case, then you should always try and look at it in a 'glass-half-full' style of thinking, gathering more info as you go along and ridding yourself of the need to assume.

Don't Condescend or Be Overly Sarcastic

Besides assumptions, other communication ticks to cut out are condescension and careless sarcasm. Being condescending means that you feel superior to those around you, and you let them know it through your patronizing style of speaking and acting. There's nothing worse than someone who talks down to you as they try to tell you just how wrong you are. This is a surefire recipe for pissing people off in the wrong way during an argument.

Similar to condescension in its ability to royally piss people off is being careless or overly sarcastic. To rebut someone's point of view with a sneer and a sarcastic answer is more likely to get you punched in the face than to win you the argument. Remember that sarcasm goes far further than the words you say. It also includes how you say it (your tone of voice) and your body language as you listen and speak. It's important to become mindful of the way that you speak to others, and to rein in any bad communication habits that you may have developed. Condescension and sarcasm are two of these.

Remember: Not Every Conversation Needs Be a Fight to the Death

The final thing to iron out if you're to develop the communication skills necessary to win any argument and start pissing people off the right way is to stop viewing every discussion or argument as a last-man-standing style of battle. Steer clear from shooting someone down with any form of personal attack. There's a big difference between disagreeing with someone's ideas or opinions and verbally attacking their person. These personal attacks include name-calling, stereotyping, intimidating, and bullying, as well as other forms of verbal abuse.

Linked to personal attacks is viewing every argument as a 'with me or against me', 'win or lose' verbal battle to the death. If you take this standpoint, you are going to end up alienating yourself from anyone who slightly disagrees with you. This often ends with both sides walking away frustrated and even more cemented in their beliefs. In other words, viewing every conversation as a fight to the death ends with both sides coming out worse rather than better for it. This is not the way to win an argument and piss people off the right way. At times, we all just have to admit that we'll never see eye-to-eye with the person we are arguing against. Doing so doesn't mean that you 'lost' the argument, but rather that you can recognize a lost cause when you see one. It also means that you are okay with some form of compromise, which is a key part of developing a winning argument style. If you find yourself intimidating your audience into silence or bullying them to agree with you, then you are definitely pissing people off in the wrong way.

And there we have it! A few beginning tips on how to start developing the communication skills necessary to win any argument. As we have seen, a winning communication style isn't one where you are overly aggressive or insult your opponent at every opportunity. This will only make people feel the need to dig in their heels and retaliate or to walk away feeling angered, humiliated, and frustrated at your rudeness. Whatever the outcome, their negative feelings will be aimed at you and your behavior rather than the subject matter you were discussing. If this happens, you have lost the argument. This doesn't mean you should steer clear of making your audience angry at all costs, but rather that you should make sure that anger is directed at the problem or pain point and not at you. Indeed, as we shall see in the next section, there can be some major benefits to pissing people off in the right way.

The Benefits of Pissing People Off

"Pissing people off is both inevitable and necessary. This doesn't mean that the goal is pissing people off. Pissing people off doesn't mean you're doing the right things, but doing the right things will almost inevitably piss people off."

— COLIN POWELL

Colin Powell, the former US Secretary of State, said it right in the quote above. If you want to get anywhere, you need to accept the fact that you're going to piss some people off along the way. This in no way means that you should go out with the aim or intent of irritating or angering people. Rather, it means you should accept the fact that, as politely and eloquently as you may speak your truth, not everyone is going to be pleased to hear it.

To begin reaping the benefits of pissing people off, you need to know the difference between aiming to do so and understanding that doing so is an inevitability often outside of your ability to control. Let's take a case study from the world of leadership. Imagine that you are in a leadership position such as, say, being the

Secretary of State. This means that you are responsible for carrying out the foreign policy for an entire country. You definitely don't want to go into any meeting with a foreign power intent on pissing them off, but you'd also be doing a massive disservice to your own country if you didn't still say your piece knowing that it may piss people off. In this situation, your job is to piss people off as diplomatically as possible. In other words, to piss people off the right way. Just as this idea works for the highest branches of government, so too does it work for every discussion or conversation you find yourself in.

The bottom line is that being a responsible member of society means that you're going to piss some individuals, or even groups of people, off at certain times. To be a pro conversationalist doesn't mean aiming to make everyone like you all the time. That makes you a pushover, not a wizard of logic and master of debates. As Colin Powell says in his speech on leadership and victory in business and life:

"Trying to get everyone to like you is a sign of mediocrity: You'll avoid the tough decisions, you'll avoid confronting the people who need to be confronted, and you'll avoid offering differential rewards based on differential performance because some people might get upset."

If you try to treat everyone the same without taking into account their "contributions", then all you'll end up doing is angering the people who you want on your side. According to Powell, these are often "the most creative and productive people in an organization." As with an organization, so with any conversation. Don't shy away from standing up for what you believe in because, chances are, there are many other people who think the same as you and will be in your corner if you prove yourself to be a skilled mouthpiece for their beliefs and opinions. What would you rather? To be criticized by people on your side and thought of indifferently by those you tried to appease, or to be criticized by the opposition but lorded by those in your corner. This is the 'benefit' of pissing people off, or, at least, why it shouldn't be avoided in conversations, discussions, and debates.

2

YOU DON'T HAVE TO BE A GENIUS

Becoming a communication king or a logic queen might seem like something reserved for the geniuses around us. For those who seem to be blessed with the gift of the gab or with an IQ that would make Einstein proud. However, I'm here to tell you that this isn't the case. Most of the time, it isn't the intelligence levels you bring to the table or the actual content of what you say that matters.

What's, oftentimes, more impactful is the context that you create for your argument and the ways in which you emphasize your points. While it's nearly impossible to increase your IQ to genius levels and is extremely difficult to learn every nuance or factoid on a particular topic, this isn't what creates a pro communicator. If you think about it, geniuses are not renowned for being the best of orators out there. This is because the genius often gets lost in the facts and figures, stumbling over their words as their brains race ahead trying to logically solve the puzzle of the conversation. The pro communicator knows that intelligence and content come in a distant second when compared to the circumstances of the conversation or argument. The pro communicator knows the real power comes from context and, as such, focuses on creating, reframing, and changing meanings to fit their argument and audience.

In this chapter, we're going to cover the importance of context in communication. We'll begin by chatting about semantics, the branch of linguistics and logic that deals with meaning and interpretation. After that, we'll go over some top communication tips and tricks that you can use to start setting the context of conversations and lead people to see things from your point of view. Using the techniques we'll cover in this chapter, you won't need to have Einstein levels of intelligence to seem like the smartest, most charismatic person in the room because, at the end of the day, 'genius' is a matter of semantics.

THE THEORY OF ARGUMENTATION

Have you heard of the term 'argumentation' before? To use the definition from Merriam-Webster, it's the "act or process of forming reasons and of drawing conclusions and applying them to a case in discussion." It deals with using semantics (how language contributes to meaning) and pragmatics (how context contributes to meaning) to create the most convincing line of argument possible. In other words, it's the way we form reasons for our beliefs, justify them, provide examples and explanations, and then draw our audience to a conclusion so powerful they can't help but be influenced by our argumentative prowess.

Argumentation vs Persuasion

Argumentation is a theory or school of thought studied by philosophers and practiced by lawyers. It's useful for anyone who deals with rhetoric (the art of persuasion), dialectic (the art of investigating opposing opinions), and logic (the art of assessing validity). We'll get more into these three disciplines in a little bit, but let's first begin with a quick chat about the difference between argumentation and persuasion.

As we just covered above, argumentation deals with persuasion through rhetoric, but that's not all that it's about. Similarly, it's tough to persuade anyone of anything without knowing a bit about how to argue your point properly, but the skill of persuasion is about more than just that. It's easiest to think about it in the form of writing. An argumentative essay, article, or speech is very different to a persuasive one. For one thing, a persuasive piece can be primarily emotive, using personal stories and powerful images to sway the audience through emotion. An argumentative piece, on the other hand, has to back up its claim with facts and figures, research and evidence. Emotion doesn't come into argumentation. Now, while we are separating persuasion and argumentation quite severely here, that's just to show you the difference between the two. To win every argument and piss people off in the right way, you'll need to use a mixture of many different methods, all of which we will cover in this book. Two of these are persuasion and argumentation.

The Goals of Argumentation

The theory of argumentation has many uses, reaching far beyond just being able to win any argument that you enter. It also teaches critical thinking and how to use correct logic, which will serve you in every aspect of your life. To develop your argumentative skills, all you have to do is practice the three elements, or goals, of argumentation. They are:

- **Identify the Situation**

  The first step of argumentation theory is to identify the setting and situation surrounding the discussion or debate. This is where you 'read' your audience and decide on the best way to win them over to your side.

- **Analyze the Flow of the Discussion**

Once you've identified the argumentation situation and decided on the best way forward, the next thing to do is analyze your audience's responses and read the flow of the conversation. To become a fluent practitioner of argumentation theory, you not only need to develop your speaking skills, but also your listening skills. You also need to have a deep understanding of body language and how to read it, which we'll get to later on in this book. While you shouldn't change your beliefs or opinions to fit the audience (your aim is to change theirs, after all), you should change up your approach if you see the audience isn't connecting with your style of argumentation.

- **Evaluate the Arguments**

The final goal of argumentation theory is to do with evaluation. As a theory that draws substantially from the idea and ideals of logic, it's important to build critical reflection and evaluation into your use of it. This means both reflecting on your own arguments, as well as those of your opponents. It's also massively beneficial to reflect on the audience's response to the content and delivery style of your argument. Once that's done, determine if you managed to influence anyone's beliefs more towards yours. Then, make improvements to your argumentative approach accordingly.

THE IMPORTANCE OF CONTEXT IN COMMUNICATION

As I'm sure you already know, we humans are a social species. Our ability to communicate and collaborate with one another has been almost as important as our ingenuity in getting us hairless apes to the top of the food chain. In fact, many ingenious moments in human history were only able to happen because some genius was able to communicate their ideas with other people in a way that those other people could understand and act upon. But, as we said at the beginning of this chapter, you don't need to be a genius to win arguments, reframe situations, and get what you want out of a situation. If you think about it, though, most geniuses aren't really renowned for their conversation skills, are they? For some, the mere thought of public speaking gives them the cold sweats. This means that it's easier for us 'Average Joes' to master the art of conversation and communication than it is for the majority of geniuses out there. If you're one of those rarities who has both the gift of the gab and the gift of genius, please use your powers to make the world a better place!

Setting the Context

From the moment we wake up until the time we fall asleep, we are constantly communicating. It could be talking to friends and family, sending a message to someone on your phone, creating or commenting on social media posts, having a chat in the coffee shop with a complete stranger, presenting to a client, sending an email updating your team; the list of possible communications we could have in a single day is endless.

Even though we are always communicating, this doesn't mean that we always do it right. At times, the communication stream flows effortlessly from communicator to receiver, with the message or aim of the conversation being clear and easy to understand. Other times, though, there seems to be nothing we can do to make the receiver understand what we are trying to say, or we receive a message that makes absolutely no sense or seems completely illogical to us. What decides the difference between the two? The context of the communication.

Putting communication in the correct context is critical for making sure that the messages we put out into the world are understood and interpreted correctly. Context lets the listener know what the reason for or importance of your communication is, and provides them with the background information necessary to accept certain assumptions dealing with the conversation topic. The best thing that context does, though, is give your message meaning, deepening and broadening the receiver's understanding and allowing for a true conversation to develop.

Let's go over some top tips on how you can start setting the context like a pro communicator in every conversation or communication that you have!

- **It Starts With Perspective**

  To begin setting the context, you first need to nail down what your audience or receiver's perspective looks like. Have you heard the quote, "Walk a mile in someone else's shoes," before? It comes from a poem called *Judge Softly,* written in 1895 by American author, preacher, and suffragist, Mary T. Lathrap. Lathrap ends her poem on the need to understand another's perspective rather than judge them with the line: "Take the time to walk a mile in his moccasins."

To step into the shoes of your audience, think about things from their point of view. Consider the way that they would interpret what you're trying to say. If you were them, what would you need to know in order to understand the context of the message you are conveying? What background information would help them to further understand what you're saying and, thereby, help to further your own agenda? Spend some time analyzing your audience and trying to figure out what their responses will be. This is how you can start setting the context and framing your argument with your audience in mind.

• Balance the Power Dynamics

Have you ever had a conversation with someone who continuously, if unknowingly, speaks over or down to people? It's the worst! And is dead certain to piss people off in the wrong way. By acting like you know more than the person you're speaking to, you put people on the defensive. This means they'll be less likely to open up, and highly unlikely to see things from your perspective, nevermind change theirs (which is our aim). It also creates an imbalance of the power dynamic in the people involved in the conversation, turning it into more of a battlefield where everyone is either vying for power, feeling threatened, or getting defensive. Rather than a battlefield, turn the conversation into a dance of which you are the maestro. Be open, see things from all points of view, and grade the complexity of your language and points according to the context and company in which you find yourself. While Albert Einstein might have been a genius not renowned to be a spectacular orator, he does have a great quote that says: "If you can't explain it to a six-year-old, then you don't understand it yourself." By this, Einstein didn't mean that you should treat every person you talk to as if they are six years old, but rather that it's not about showing what you know about something. Rather, it's about ensuring the person, or people, you're talking to are able to understand what you're trying to say. This is how you become the balancer of the power dynamics, and the maestro of the dance that is a conversation.

- **Solve Their Pain Points**

There's a term in marketing and business known as the 'pain point'. This is the problem that the customer has that is solved by the product or service a business provides. If you are to master the art of setting the context in a conversation, you need to learn how to hone in on your audience's pain points. We covered a major pain point in the point above when we mentioned how it pisses people off in the wrong way when someone acts like they know more than the person they're talking to, and doesn't share that information. Feeling like they are left out of the loop or that they don't know some important piece of information is one pain point you can start solving for your 'customers' today. Providing an answer to your audience's pains, problems, and fears allows you to win them over through removing ambiguity and anxiety from their lives.

- **Be Proactive**

Linked to honing in on your audience's pain points is addressing them in a proactive manner. Doing so will help your audience to see the benefit of listening to you, help them to process what you've got to say faster, and make decisions or take action which is more in-line with your agenda than their initial one was. It's important to be proactive when communicating in context. The goal is to try to anticipate the questions your audience may think and to ask or answer them before they think to raise it in the conversation. Through doing so, you'll make people feel like you just 'get them', helping them to feel relaxed, comfortable, and ensuring that they're primed for reaching the conclusion you have planned for them.

And there you have it! A theory that will make you seem like a genius (argumentation), and proof that you don't need to be a genius to be a pro communicator. You just need to practice putting your audience first and know how to set the context of the communication. In the next chapter, we'll move on to how to enhance your creative and critical thinking skills through learning the difference between a map and a territory as we discover the power of mind mapping. Let's go!

3

MIND MAPPING

Mistaking the map for the territory. Believe it or not, this is what a lot of people do. Not literally, of course, but in terms of the way they see their own 'map' of reality rather than the thing itself. That 'map' is our internalized perception of the world around us, our beliefs, and our interpretation of reality. In a way, we all rely on our own maps to make sense of the world around us. In other words, there is no perfect, all-encompassing map or version of reality. A bit deep for Chapter 3, I know, but bear with me.

By its nature, a map is only a representation and will always fall short of being completely accurate or realistic. As with the map, so with our view of reality. The five senses through which we experience the world around us—sight, hearing, touch, smell, and taste—sends sensory information through our nervous system to our brains, which then use that info to create a representation of the world around us, according to the data it has received, complete or not. What does this have to do with winning arguments and pissing people off in the right way, you may ask. Well, first of all, it allows you to step outside of the box of only having one map of reality. This allows you to control, and even choose, how you see the world, as well as to easily see and interpret things from someone else's point of view, which, as we saw in the previous chapter, is a key part of setting the context of the communication. Secondly, it frees you of the logical fallacy known as 'mistaking the map for the territory'.

In this chapter, we're going to go over the main ways you can start separating the territory that is reality from the mental map that is your sensory representation of it. We'll outline why it's considered a logical fallacy to mistake the map for the territory before moving on to how you can create your own mental map of reality using mind-mapping.

OF MENTAL MAPS AND REAL TERRITORIES

As we mentioned above, mistaking the map for the territory is a common logical fallacy that many people fall for, often without even knowing it. This kind of flawed logic or argumentative error usually takes place when a person confuses the semantics of a word (what it means) with the thing it represents (what it really is). By 'logical fallacy', we mean some error in logic that stops your argument from being logically sound. This doesn't mean the argument isn't persuasive and can't sway the minds and hearts of your audience. It does mean, though, that you are going to come up second-best to someone who is aware of the fallacy, and won't be able to poke holes in the arguments of those that fall prey to it, too. So, my pro orator in the making, that is why learning about such logical fallacies is important for those looking to win every argument and piss people off in the right way. Separating the 'map' from the 'territory' is also a freeing way to think of communication and life in general. Let's begin with the explanation.

Re-map to Increase Your Options

If you take to heart that every map is, by its very nature, only an inaccurate summary of the territory it represents, you have taken the first step towards increasing the options available to you in any conversation or communication. This is because it allows you to take a step back, separate yourself from your mental map of reality, and remap to the context you find yourself in and/or are trying to set. Remapping takes the idea of viewing things from a different perspective to the next level and is a great technique for winning arguments. Through viewing things from your audience's 'map', you'll also know how to piss them off in just the right way so that they love you all the more for it.

Remember that everyone creates their maps of reality through their five senses. In neuro-linguistic programming (NLP) terms, these are called our 'representational systems'. It's through our internal senses that we 're-present' (present again) the external world. While it's impossible for you to fully see the mental map of the person you're talking to (you can't know every experience that they've had, after all), you can build a map of them as the conversation develops.

Ways to Start Separating the Map From the Territory

Understanding the difference between the map and the territory gives you the freedom to draw your own maps and make them as large-scale or localized as you want or need in a certain context. It increases your options in any given situation to no end, with your imagination being the only limit. Let's go over a few top tips on how to analyze your audience and ensure you are tailoring the map of the conversation in a way that perfectly fits their own representation of reality.

It's All in the Eyes

Whoever said, "The eyes are the window to the soul," was on to something. I'd change it up a bit for this book, though, and say, "The eyes are the window to your audience's mental map." We talk a lot more with our bodies than many people give credit. These are the people uninitiated in the ways of neuro-linguistic programming though, and as such, aren't me, and soon, won't be you either.

In NLP, body language related to the eyes and eye patterns are called 'eye accessing cues'. Although there's still quite a bit of conjecture as to whether eye accessing cues are universal or not, there are some main ones that are thought to be 'common. These are:

- **Upwards for Visuals**

   When people look upwards, they are visualizing something. If their eyes briefly move upwards during a conversation, they are letting you know they can imagine what you are saying and are keeping up with you and the conversation. When a person's eyes move up and to the left, it's a cue that they're remembering visuals, drawing on things they have seen and experienced. When a person's eyes move up and to the right, this is a cue that they are creating visuals rather than remembering them.

- **Level for Auditory**

When someone is staring straight-on, this is a sign they are processing auditory information. If you look straight and to the left, you are remembering sounds, while level and to the right means you are creating sounds. Constructed audio includes things like asking your audience to imagine the sound of pages turning or the wind rustling through leaves.

- **Down and Right for Kinesthetic**

If the person you're speaking to looks down and to the right, this is a sign that they're accessing their inner emotions or feelings. By extension, it could also mean that the person you're speaking to has understood what you're saying, is processing what you have said, or is connecting to your message.

• Down and Left for Internal Dialogue

The final common eye pattern is looking down and left, which is a sign that a person is speaking to themselves. Also known as 'internal dialogue', this often means that the person you're talking to isn't focusing or listening intently, because they are busy having a discussion with themselves.

As you can see, the eyes are indeed a window into the inner workings of a person's thoughts, feelings, and connections with your message or what you are speaking about. Now that you know about these common eye patterns, you don't only have to use them in observation, but can use them to bring on certain thought processes. Want to create an imaginary situation or hypothetical circumstance? Look top right. Want to remember some image or event from your past? Look top left. It's the same with auditory and kinesthetic processes, and even with bringing on a state of internal dialogue. With NLP, you can use it to not only read your audience better, but to also read yourself better and learn to set the context that brings on a certain state, internal or external. It's also one helluva great way to begin separating the map from the territory.

Learn to be an Active Listener

After the eyes, the next best way to tailor the map to fit your audience's representation of reality is to develop the skill of listening. Most of us think that we listen to someone else when they talk, but what we're really doing is thinking of what we're going to say next. It's a natural human thing to do because we place more importance on what we have to say compared to what someone is saying to us. It's our map through which we see, hear, feel, taste, and touch reality, after all, not someone else's. This is the viewpoint of someone who confuses the map for the territory and, as such, isn't for me and isn't for you. Rather than always thinking how you can fit what someone is saying into your representation, think about how what they're saying tells you more about their world view and how you can use this to better tailor what you're saying to get the result you're after.

The way to become an active listener is to practice being fully present in a conversation. Focus on what the other person has to say and actively *listen*. When we listen to what someone is saying during a conversation, there are always two goals. The first is to take in the overt meaning of what the person is saying and understand the emotion behind their words. The second is to show interest, engage with the meaning of their words, and display a general care for what the other person has to say. If you are just doing the first part, you're failing the task of actively listening, and the same with if you only do the second. It takes two to tango, just as it takes you being both a speaker and a listener in conversation as you dance out a dialogue with your conversation partner, or partners.

Linked to the two goals we mentioned above are the three aspects of active listening. They are:

- **Cognitive**

    The cognitive aspect deals with the brain and the intake of information. This is the part that most people associate with listening but goes a bit deeper than the simple description given in the sentence before. When we pay attention to what people are saying, we take in both the explicit (external) and implicit (internal) meaning to their words, comprehend the message as a whole, and work this information into the context of the conversation and your surroundings.

- **Emotional**

After the cognitive comes the emotional. This doesn't mean breaking down, crying, ranting, or raving while the other person is telling you their tale. Quite the opposite, in fact. To be an effective active listener, we need to become aware of our emotional responses and learn to control them. Be cool, stay calm, and portray compassion rather than annoyance or boredom when someone is speaking to you.

- **Behavioral**

Linked to the emotional aspect of active listening is the behavior. Just as you should manage your emotional responses during a conversation, so should you manage your physical reactions while listening to someone. It goes beyond just controlling your reactions, though, to knowing how to convey interest both verbally and through body language, for example, but more on this later.

Being an active listener is an important part of determining the context in any situation, and vital in your attempts to separate the map from the territory.

This is because it forces you to focus on the other person and their 'map' rather than your own, but you can just as easily use what we just covered to determine if your audience is actively listening to you while you speak, too. If not, maybe change up your approach until what you're saying hits them just right and they can't help but be enthralled.

Read the Language of the Body

As we mentioned above, body language is a massively important part of learning how to read and set the context of the conversation. Learning how to read body language is also an essential skill for anyone looking to piss people off in the right way. If you want to become a lean, mean, argument-winning machine, you'll need to develop a deep understanding of body language and how to read even a person's most subtle cues, such as their breathing patterns and the tenseness of their muscles. We're not going to go that deep over here, but rather provide you with a few useful pointers on how to start using body language to perfect the art of active listening.

- **Look Like a Listener**

    This might be a no-brainer, but I'm going to say it anyway: To be an active listener, you need to look like you are actively listening. As good as you may be at listening to someone while doing other things, that is more passive listening than active listening and, besides, is sure to piss the person speaking off in the wrong way. Think of the phrase "pay attention". You are paying the person speaking to you with your attention. Make sure you get your money's worth! Avoid checking your phone while someone else is speaking and try not to even look at your watch. Once you start paying attention to it, you'll quickly realize just how distracted most people in the world are. You'll also realize how much more people open up and bond with you if you actively pay attention to what they've got to say. To look like a listener, focus on the person speaking by literally turning your head and torso to directly face them. Next, make eye contact with them, but not so much that it gets uncomfortable. A general rule of thumb is that you should maintain eye contact for as long as it takes you to notice their eye color. After that, you could maintain eye contact until you notice the eye pattern or direction that their eyes are in. Finally, lean forward so that you show you are engaging with what they are saying and want to hear more.

- **Open Up**

If you want people to open up to you, make sure that your body language indicates that you are being open. Opening up your body language has a lot to do with your posture and the way that you hold yourself. The opposite of an open posture is a closed posture. This is when someone crosses their legs or folds their arms, turning their torso away from the conversation. Touching your face regularly or hiding your hands away are also two indicators of closed body language.

In order to have an open body posture, keep your legs uncrossed when sitting and slightly apart when standing, feet flat on the floor. Keep your arms relaxed and hanging at your side with your hands in sight. Also, use gestures where you show your palms facing up, as this is a sign that you are inviting the person to carry on the conversation. Finally, tilt your head toward the person slightly, signaling that you're interested in what the person is saying, curious about what they could say next, or are still actively listening to the story or idea they are telling you about.

- **Smile**

Some of the most powerful weapons in your body language repertoire are facial expressions. Out of these, the most potent one is the smile. There is nothing more disarming, comforting, or trust-inducing than a genuine smile. Not only do smiles make us seem more approachable and willing to cooperate, but they also make us as the smilers feel great. It's very hard not to smile at someone when they smile at you. Try it for yourself, if you don't believe me. Make sure that you don a genuine smile when you do this activity though!

An authentic smile begins at the corners of the eyes, crinkling up as the corners of your mouth slowly raise, drawing your mouth into a smile that enlightens your whole face and fades as slowly as it was raised. A genuine smile is a superpower when it comes to conversation skills and active listening. As we said, smiling makes the smiler feel great as it stimulates feelings of comfort and wellbeing. However, it's very hard to stop yourself from smiling when someone smiles at you. So, smile at the person speaking, they'll smile back, you'll both feel great, and connect over this feeling of wellbeing that is a smile.

- **Mirror to Increase Agreeability**

The final body basic body language technique that you can use to enhance your active listening is to mirror the body language of the person that is speaking. When we do this, our bodies are telling the other person that we like them, feel comfortable around them, and/or agree with what they're saying. Think of mirroring as listening and responding to the non-verbal part of the conversation as you get in-tune with what the other person's body is saying.

Most of us naturally mirror the facial expressions, postures, and even gestures of our friends and people we are comfortable around. All that we need to do is become conscious of this and use it sparingly and subtly during a conversation to show the other person that you are comfortable around them and that they, therefore, should feel comfortable around you, too.

Body language basics out of the way, we now come to the end of this section here. It's been a wild ride of learning to separate the map from the territory. After that, we went a few steps further as we learned to re-map and set the territory (i.e., the context) of any conversation. As we have seen, re-mapping has a lot to do with focusing on the mental maps of other people (their representation of reality and how they interact with it). Through learning to read, and give off, the subtle signs that sway those you converse with into feeling comfortable and open around you, we can prime our audience for changing the way they represent reality or, at the very least, know when we've pissed them off just enough to be loved for it.

A MAPPING OF MINDS

Now that we've separated the map from the territory, it's time to focus on how to map out your own path to successfully winning every argument you enter and being loved all the more for it. We use a tried and tested technique to do this, one that I'm sure you've come into contact with more than a few times in your life, if only at school. The technique I'm talking about is mind mapping. Yes, you heard me; that diagram with your idea in the central circle and lines connecting to it with the different details linked to your main idea. A good ol' brainstorm. That said, the science behind mind-mapping goes a whole lot deeper than you think.

A mind map can be thought of as a visual representation of how our brain and neocortex function. In simpler terms, this means that our brains start with a central idea or notion. This is then branched out into sub-ideas as it goes down the neocortex line. These then branch out again and again depending on the complexity and detail of the idea. Understanding this concept allows us to make changes and take control of the more specific details, contexts, and circumstances; to create our own 'mind-maps' in the conversations we enter, branching out our ideas as far as is needed to convince our readers that we know what we're talking about and they should believe us. Let's take a closer look into this powerful tool for taking control of not only the conversation but, more importantly, your own mind.

Why Is Mind Mapping So Powerful?

To put it simply, a mind map is one of the best organizational thinking tools around. It allows us to map out our thoughts and remember long and complex pieces of information. Believe me, if you want to start winning arguments, you need to know what you're talking about and have points to back up your claim. This just goes with the territory of argumentation and persuasion: You have to know what you're talking about. In the past, you could get far pretending to know what you're talking about, but in the modern day, someone can easily just pick up their phone during a conversation and fact-check your claim before believing you. There's nothing more harmful to winning an argument than being labeled a liar or, to use a popular term, "fake news". As such, it's important to have a lot of real examples and actual explanations ready to back up your claim. Luckily, there's no need to write a whole essay or even read a book on the matter (although it's always recommended to read up on your areas of interest). Just take out a piece of paper, draw a central circle, plonk your topic in the middle, and then do a bit of research, connecting some interesting tidbits of information to your central circle as you find it on the web. Read over it once or twice, and you'll have those examples and argument points memorized, primed, and ready to be used to sway your audience during a conversation.

Beyond just helping you to become the smartest person in the room, mind mapping also helps to invigorate critical and creative thinking, structure ideas, heighten memorization and concentration, and even aid with making decisions and planning your way to overcoming any difficulties that you may be facing. Overall, it's a good idea to add to your argumentor's toolbox. Let's go over why exactly it is that mind maps are so powerful.

- **They Create a Map of Your Thoughts**

The first reason why mind maps are so powerful is because they map out our thoughts using a similar structure to the way the original thought happened in the brain. Our brain is one massive connection of neurons, billions of them. All neurons (aka 'nerve cells') connect with one another, forming a neural network or neural web. There are central nuclei, the neuron, that has thousands of branches, known as 'dendrites', leading out from it, many even connecting to the dendrites of other neurons. In other words, our brains are nothing more than a massive mind map, and it's a powerful thing to bring to any brainstorming exercise.

- **Color Stimulates the Brain**

If you thought you were going to make your mind maps in black and white, I've got other news for you. Monochrome is very monotonous for the brain, while color and vibrancy stimulate it. We literally get energized by seeing bright colors. So, make your mind maps colorful and you'll further enhance the amount of information that you manage to retain and that you can recall at a moment's notice.

- **A Collaboration of Different Thinking Methods**

Another unique thing about mind maps is that they combine a lot of different types of thinking. As we mentioned above, it's best to make your mind maps colorful. Added to the drawing factor, this activates our artistic and creative thinking. As we covered earlier, it's a representation of the way that we have ideas and make connections, which makes it an organizational science. Through creating connections between different ideas, we also activate our logical and critical thinking skills. Combine that with both words and images, as well as emotions, through colors and drawings, and you've got one potent think-tank of a technique.

- **They Help Us Generate Ideas and Notice Patterns**

The final superpower of mind maps is in helping us to draw connections between different points and even notice patterns in a single idea or between multiple different points. This part of mind mapping comes more from when you read over and analyze the map again rather than when you create it for the first time. Because it's not meant to be a one-and-done kind of job. Mind maps are generative, which means that they help us to generate new ideas through analyzing what we already know, noticing gaps or patterns in our logic, thereby improving and deepening our understanding of the topic. For memorization, understanding, and thinking over information, a mind map has you covered.

Creating Mind Maps

Although making a mind map is pretty easy, there is a bit more to it than you may think, especially if you want to get the most out of it. The mind mapping process that we're going to go over below comes from the renowned neuroscientist and communication pathologist, Dr. Caroline Leaf, and is one that works no matter the depth or complexity of the idea that you want to map out. Let's get your mind-mapping game on point!

• It's All About the Input

Making a mind map is part of the planning or researching stage of development. As such, you need to know what you are researching, and research it. The mind map should be the summary of the info that you read, listen, or watch. A general rule of thumb is that you should select about 15-35% from what you research and use this as the input for your mind map. Focus on a specific part of the research material rather than the entire thing; you can always create another mind map to deal with the other factors of the reading.

• Create the Mind Map

With your input information selected and at the ready, now comes the time to design your mind map. Get your blank paper at the ready and draw your central circle, adding as much artistry as you are capable of to make it unique and easily memorable. For me, there ain't much art going on in my mind maps, but I try my best to add a scribble or sketch every now and then to make it personal and to aid my ability to recall the mind-mapped information (through remembering the specific type of mind map itself).

- **Reflect, Personalize, and Teach**

After you have created your mind map comes the time to read over the summarized information and reflect on it. This is also a great time to add more color and flare to your mind map. Trust me, the more visually appealing the map is, the easier it will be to recall it and re-present the information embedded in it.

Another great way to improve your ability to remember the mind-mapped information is to discuss it with, or teach it to, someone. This will help to take the info from being stored in your short-term memory and upgrade to your long-term memory stores. If you can't find an actual person willing to let you 'teach' them or don't have a discussion buddy, no problem! Just teach it to your pet, your child, or even your house plant. Another option is to look into the mirror and teach yourself, or to imagine a person and teach them. Whatever and whoever you choose matters far less than the action of teaching back the information. Through this process, you won't just store the information in your brain, but start to link it with other mind maps, integrate it with discussion or argument points, and apply it in helping you win every argument you enter.

Welcome, argument king or queen in the making, to the end of Chapter 3! So far, we've been setting the stage for how to win arguments and piss people off the right way. We've learned the basics of effective communication and the importance of reading and setting the context of the conversation. As we've seen, in order to read the context of the discussion, you first need to separate the map from the territory. Only through doing so will you be able to read the map of your audience and the context in which the argument or conversation is taking place. We then went over the basics of body language and how to read it as we learned about the importance of being an active listener.

It's not all about reading the room and listening to your audience, though; you also need to impress them with what you know. That's where research and mind mapping come into play. A mind map is the perfect planning tool for us to use in our pursuit of winning every argument. It's quick to make, easy to populate, and visually appealing for our brains. It also reflects the way thoughts and ideas are stored in the brain, which you can reverse-engineer during a debate or discussion to create a mental map of your argument points in the minds of your audience.

In the next chapter, we're going to deepen your connection to your audience and your ability to influence their thoughts as we talk about the importance of feelings and the value of emotionally intelligent arguing.

4

EMOTIONAL RESCUE

Emotion plays a huge part in the way that we humans see, understand, and experience the world around us. While the pure follower of argumentation theory might want to leave emotion out of the picture completely, that's not the way to win every argument. As we said back in Chapter 2, the best way to win arguments and piss people off the right way is to use a combination of argumentation theory's flawless logic and persuasion's potent emotive responses.

Just as emotions are an unavoidable part of being human, so is having arguments, disagreeing with others, and debating contentious issues. Should we keep quiet and not voice our opinions because they are different or completely the opposite to someone else's in the conversation? Hell no! Should we shout everyone down with the words "You're wrong, I'm right!" and get into verbal fisticuffs at the slightest disagreement? Of course not! It takes a balanced and well-rounded individual to tread the line of the conversation, standing up for themselves while simultaneously winning over their audience, pissing them off because they can't help but change their beliefs based on their argumentative rationale and persuasive prowess. It takes a person knowing how to read a room, set the context, and connect with their audience on a behavioral, intellectual, and emotional level.

In the previous chapter, we covered the behavioral side, as we learned to separate the map from the territory and how to be an active listener, and the intellectual side as we covered mind mapping. In this chapter, we're going to go over the emotional side as we learn about emotional intelligent arguing and why emotions are more persuasive than logic. Let's go!

EMOTIONALLY INTELLIGENT ARGUING

Believe it or not, our inability to see eye to eye is built into our very physiology. A study carried out by the Institute of Cognitive Neuroscience at University College London found that there are marked anatomical differences between the brain of a liberal and the brain of a conservative. Crazy, right? This doesn't mean that it's impossible to change our way of thinking, but rather that some beliefs or opinions are so deeply ingrained in our psyches that we don't even realize they're there. If you run the same train of thought over and over again, you're going to leave a track of it in the neural pathways of your brain. The more you think about that idea (and the certain viewpoint you have of it), the more enhanced and deepened the connection between the neurons becomes. It's important to understand this in order to overcome it.

What do you do when you come up against someone whose opinions are so different to yours, but who is also so ingrained in their beliefs that they refuse, or even mock, seeing things from your perspective? This is where emotionally intelligent arguing comes into play. If you know how to manage and control your emotions, then you can remain in-control of yourself and continue to set the correct context for winning arguments and pissing people off the right way. When we allow our emotions to run rampant during an argument or disagreement, it tends to end in the conversation going nowhere very quickly. This won't win you the argument. All it leads to are both sides hunkering down and getting ready for battle, verbal or otherwise.

How to Become an Emotionally Intelligent Arguer

The emotionally intelligent arguer views things through the lenses of rationality and productivity. Someone using this technique is not only much more certain to win over their audience, but also to strengthen the relationships you have with people, even if they disagree with you. Over time, these people will come over to your side, because you are always in control during a discussion and, with your knowledge of body language and the added knowledge you spread (easily remembered courtesy of the mind maps), you will always seem like the smartest person in the room, without being arrogantly so. When you remain calm during a heated discussion, it immediately cools it off. It shows that you respect the person that you disagree with and are actively listening to them.

Let's go over the main ways you can keep an emotional level-head even in the most heated of arguments, and how you can add emotionally intelligent arguing to your repertoire of argumentative and persuasive skills. Remember that the goal isn't to be emotion-free, but to be in control of your emotions.

• The Power of Questions

As we covered when we talked about active listening, communication is always made up of at least two, the speaker and the listener, with the roles interchanging as the conversation flows on. While most people may only focus on what they want to say next in the discussion, this isn't for a toastmaster such as yourself. You understand that people want to be listened to; yearn to be heard. This is never more so than in a heated argument. Do either of these sound familiar? "Let me finish!" or, worse still, "You're not even listening to me!"

These are phrases said in the heat of battle, when tempers are flaring, and the conversation is slowly smoldering into a raging inferno. To combat this and save the conversation from burning out or ending up in a fist fight, make sure that the person you are talking to feels heard. Doing this is simple; just ask them a question about their viewpoint or to expand or elaborate on what they just said. This will not only catch them off guard but can also go a long way toward changing their way of thinking. A great question perfectly placed in a conversation can help someone reach the conclusion that their viewpoint is wrong without you ever having to tell them that. Don't focus on your feelings too much (you already know who you are and how you feel about things), but rather act like a journalist (the good kind) trying to understand the point of view of the person you're talking to.

• Listen Rather Than Plan

As we've mentioned before, most people don't actively listen to what the other person is saying. They're too busy planning their next killer comeback or a rebuttal sure to knock the socks off of their opponent, but when they force their chance to speak and announce their undeniable truth, it falls on deaf ears. Their opponent isn't listening either but is already lost in planning out what they're going to say next. Break the cycle through actively listening to your 'opponent' rather than planning out your next move. You've already mind-mapped your argument points out to be implemented at a moment's notice, so focus instead on the other person and how you can change their opinion to better match yours. As you actively listen to your opponent during an argument or conversation, you'll soon see them start doing the same and taking in what you've got to say. When this happens, your audience is receptive to what you've got to say, and you can lay out your mind-mapped argument points on ears that will actually hear and take in that information.

- **Explain Your Way of Thinking**

Just as important as thinking about things from the perspective of the people you're talking to is getting them to see things from your perspective. This is where you show off your communication skills, describing your thoughts, beliefs, and ideas in a vivid, but simple, way that is understood and enjoyed by all. To do this, you need to simply ask yourself: "How can I best help my audience to understand my perspective?" Write it in the middle of a page, circle that bad boy, and make a mind map out of it. You may want to make another mind map with the question: "What's my perspective?" as its focus. You can grow it out from there to zoom in on your perspective for each of your different argument topics. Combine that with the information you research and how best to help your listener see things from your perspective on this matter, and you're onto a winning formula for argumentative success.

Explaining your way of thinking also shows your audience that you respect them, and, in turn, they will feel more comfortable around you and respect you the more for it.

• Play the Long Game

Changing someone's opinion or way of thinking doesn't always happen during the course of a single conversation, especially if it gets a bit heated toward the end. Rather than pushing an argument to its boiling point, display your emotional intelligence and know when to call it a day on a certain topic. This doesn't mean that you've lost the argument, especially since you'll be ending it because the other side is losing their cool. In your calm, composed manner of a context-setter and pro communicator, say that you think it would be best to call the discussion for the day. Tell them you'll reflect on what they've said, as you hope they do with your talking points, and that the conversation can continue at a later date. Then, actually reflect on their points; map them out and see if there's any common ground or workable territory for you to politely exploit in your next encounter. When you are ready, contact the person and see if they're ready to have the next discussion. Even if they say "no", you'll have gone up tenfold in their books for following up, and they're sure to listen to you far more actively the next time you meet.

EMOTIONS TRUMP LOGIC

As much as we may wish it wasn't so, logic almost always comes second when emotion is involved. There's no point denying it, and once accepted, we can start using this to our advantage. Bring both the facts and the feelings to the table, and you're onto a power-house combo of persuasiveness. Another harsh reality is that humans are not nearly as rational as we like to believe. Take smoking, for example. We know it's bad for us, we understand the facts and see the logic of that, but still, we light another one up, nodding our heads and saying "Yeah, these things are terrible for you," before taking another sweet drag. Not a smoker? It's just one example of many but goes to a central point: Humans can understand every part of the logic of something, but that's not enough of a motivation to get someone to change their beliefs. You have to add that essential emotional angle to it.

Emotional Do's and Don'ts

A study carried out by neuroscientist Antoine Bechara at the University of Iowa showed that patients who couldn't feel emotions struggled to make decisions.

These are people who've suffered orbitofrontal damage (damage to the front part of their brain immediately above the eyes).

Bechara uses a theory called the 'Somatic Harper Hypothesis' to show the neurological link between the disconnection these patients have with emotions and feelings, and their dire impairment of sound judgment and their inability to make decisions. What does this mean for you and your aim to win every argument that you enter? Well, if the emotionless can't make decisions or life choices, then those that are full of emotion must be primed to make these types of decisions. First, we learn to control our own emotions, and then we learn how to use the emotions of others in order to further set the context of the conversation and further our chances of not only winning the argument but winning them over to our point of view.

Here are a few emotional do's and don'ts that you can use as guidelines when navigating your listeners through the new territory of the conversation, adding to their mental maps as you engage and enthrall their mind, body, and emotion.

• Choose Your Emotion Wisely

When using emotion to win an argument, don't focus on a wide array of emotions, but hone in on a few select ones or, even better, a single emotion. You could focus on anger and get them riled up about the injustice of the world and connected to your argument point, of course. You could use humor to include a wider audience in the discussion and get people engaged in the conversation. Or, you could focus on inspiring people to take action. Which one you choose comes from when you are actively listening and 'reading the room' of the people you're conversing with and beginning to read and set the context.

• Steer Clear of Fear

One emotion you don't want to use is fear. Shared worries, yes. Collective pain points, definitely, but never fear. Well, only in very specific circumstances that are so uncommon that it's better to just say never. Fear may get people to take action, but that action is often frantic, illogical, and comes from a place of self-protection rather than being won over by your argumentative prowess. If you use fear to win an argument, then it is fear itself that has won, not you. Your job as a pro communicator should be to allay the fears of your audience by showing them a way out, rather than how far down they are.

• Develop a Memorable Style of Speech

I don't know about you, but when I think of emotions, I think of drama, which leads me to acting. Maybe that's just my mental mind map of that information link, but it covers an important point. If we want people to remember us and what we have to say, we have to put on a show. It's not full acting, as you want to connect with your audience on a personal basis rather than putting on a facade. Think of it more like yourself, your own personality, but enhanced, enlarged, accentuated whenever you enter into a conversation or discussion.

Animate your discussion points with gestures, paint vivid pictures with your descriptions and metaphors, and speak like you are the host of a party. If you are to set the context of the conversation, then you are, in fact, hosting that conversation. And so, take that part of your persona labeled 'host' and upgrade its mental map by adding 'host of the conversation' to the list of times it activates. If you are entertaining both in terms of what you say and how you say it and animate it, then people are far more likely to listen to, and remember, your message. Everybody loves a good show, after all!

With that, another chapter comes to an end. In this one, we learned how to bring emotion to the table in our conversations, discussions, and arguments, discussing the ins and outs of emotionally intelligent arguing before diving into how you can use emotion to best effect in driving home your message. In the next chapter, we'll be taking our knowledge of emotions to the next level as we learn about the power it has to leave a lasting influence on your audience.

5

CONVINCER AND BELIEVER

Where do your beliefs come from? While it can be difficult to answer this question, especially with the more embedded, ingrained ones, the bottom-line is that our beliefs have to come from somewhere. They definitely don't appear out of thin air, and we don't carry them over from whatever space comes before birth. In fact, there is quite a specific process by which we gain our beliefs. In order for our minds to accept a belief, it needs to pass the gauntlet of fitting into the way we see and understand the world around us. As such, it needs to link with what we already believe in, meshing together with sensory information to create the overall map that is our representation of reality.

Even if we understand that the map is not the territory and focus instead on setting the context of the discussion, we still cannot escape our beliefs. And why should we? Winning an argument doesn't mean that you believe in nothing but defeating the logic of your opponent, but rather sharing your beliefs and opinions, backed up with facts, explanations, and examples in a passionate and emotionally intelligent way that convinces the listener to change what they believe in, even if ever so slightly.

Many people go through life lost within their own minds. They never learn to read their own mental maps, let alone write their own version of it. These individuals let their emotional states control them, sabotaging themselves through stubbornly holding on to their self-limiting or past beliefs. Developing the willpower to believe something new or different seems impossible to these people, and indeed it may be. When coming up against such people, it may be best at times to just label them as a 'hopeless case' and move your focus on to people that you can actually engage with. But, if you want to slug it out with such people, the only thing that's going to work is to persuade them through emotion.

No matter how hard-lined or flexible the beliefs of the person you're talking to are, emotion is your best bet for winning them over. In this chapter, we're going to learn about the power that emotion has in influencing your audience and how to use it to get them to not only remember your message, but to take action and change their own beliefs based on what you had to say.

THE THREE KEYS OF PERSUASION

An easy analogy is to think of emotion as a key that unlocks your audience and opens them up to considering new possibilities. The art of persuasion, also known as 'rhetoric', has been studied and written about since the days of the Ancient Greek philosophers over 2,000 years ago. One of the first people to write on this topic was Aristotle, in his philosophical piece, the *Rhetoric*. In this groundbreaking piece of work, Aristotle covers three key strategies for persuading someone. They are:

- **Ethos**

  Meaning 'character', ethos covers everything to do with the person speaking and their credibility or authority as a speaker. This includes the facts that you bring to the table, as well as the way you present the information and yourself. Body language and active listening also fall under ethos.

- **Logos**

The Greek word for 'logic', this strategy deals with research, evidence, and argumentation. It's where you back up your claims with facts and figures and lay out your argument points in a way that shows you have analyzed all sides of the situation before reaching the deductions you are telling them about.

- **Pathos**

The final persuasion strategy laid out by Aristotle was pathos, the Greek word for 'experience'. You've seen the word pathos before, just in its modern forms. These are the words 'sympathy' and 'empathy'. By 'pathos', Aristotle meant the experience you create that leads to persuasion. In other words, the context that you set and the emotions you get your audience to feel.

BEING EMOTIONALLY PERSUASIVE

In this section, we're going to focus on the pathos; the emotional experience you create and use to persuade your audience to change their beliefs in favor of yours. Remember, nothing we've looked at so far should be done by itself. You need to incorporate all of the skills and techniques we've covered in every conversation. The next skill to add to your repertoire is to master the art of persuading through engaging the emotional response of your audience. Let's go over how exactly you can do so.

Tell a Story

All humans have a powerful response to a great story. It's built into our brains, into our psyche, to enjoy hearing someone weave a tale of successes and failures, adventures and revelations. There are even some who say that we humans are nothing more than storytelling animals (check out the book 'The Storytelling Animal' by Jonathan Gottschall to find out more about this). When we listen to a good story, we become emotionally invested in what the person has to say. When this happens, your audience is primed for persuasion.

Make Use of Figurative Language

Linked to telling a good story is to use similes and metaphors during your conversations and debates. A simile is when we compare one thing to another using words like 'like' or 'as…as'. This can help to draw connections between what you're saying and something the audience is familiar with and, hopefully, feels strongly for or about. Think of similes that would bring to life an interesting connection in your audience's mind.

A metaphor is when we equate one thing to something else. "Time is money," for example, or, "the world's a stage." Even, "the eyes are the window to the soul," is a metaphor. We use metaphors to once again spark off an interesting connection in your audience's mind, to provide more color or clarity for your argument point, or to highlight a strong similarity between two different ideas.

Both similes and metaphors are great ways to get emotional responses from your audience and are a lot quicker to use than telling a whole story. Although, for the ultimate effect, you should use similes and metaphors inside of your stories.

Be Personal

The next step to becoming more emotionally persuasive is to be as personal as you can be. This is not only in terms of how you speak and present yourself, but also in terms of what you've got to say. There's nothing that closes the gap between you and your audience more than when you get vulnerable in front of them. For most people, being vulnerable and open can feel akin to getting naked in front of someone, but if you can get comfortable with brazenly baring all, you'll have a powerful emotional persuasion skill under your proverbial belt. To share your own experiences and open up during a conversation encourages your audience to do exactly the same.

Being personal isn't something that you can fake, and you shouldn't need to. All you've got to do is be passionate about what you believe in. Let your audience know your hopes and dreams and draw links between your argument points and your lived experience that gave root to them. Add this to active listening and setting the context and you're onto a persuasive formula for winning every argument, as well as for winning people over to your side.

6

NEURO-LINGUISTIC PROGRAMMING

With your background knowledge complete, you are now ready to take your conversation game to the next level with neuro-linguistic programming. We've touched on a few topics that fall under the heading of 'neuro-linguistics', such as body language, active listening, and setting the context, but now's the time to get under the hood and see what really makes a conversation tick.

In this chapter, we're going to cover the history and uncover the mystery that is neuro-linguistic programming; the way that you talk to others and yourself and how it affects the context of the conversation and its outcome. Using the techniques we're about to cover, you'll not only become a master communicator, but also learn how to talk to yourself using language that empowers you to change unwanted habits, rid yourself of limiting beliefs, and become a goal-oriented, driven person. All the successful people of the world are doing it, so why not you? Read on to find out how, but first, a lil' bit of history.

THE ORIGINS OF NLP

Neuro-linguistic programming is a combination of psychology and linguistics. Which makes sense, considering that it was a psychologist and a linguist who first thought up the field of study now known as 'NLP'. It was the early 1970s, in Santa Cruz, California, when Richard Bandler, a psychology student, started to talk to John Grinder, associate professor of linguistics at UC Santa Cruz, about how some people seemed to fit the label of 'successful person', while others did not. Bandler, who had begun his studies majoring in math and computer science, approached it from a formulaic angle; they were typing in the right code. Grinder brought a more linguistic-based approach and looked at it from a language point-of-view. Soon, the two reached the conclusion that language, and how the successful people used it, was fundamentally and startlingly different to their less successful brothers and sisters. While successful people used language that encouraged themselves and everyone else, the less successful did not. Very soon, the two were so invested that Bandler left behind the world of math and computer science and changed his degree to behavioral science (which he would later get his PhD in). The psychologist and the linguist set to work creating their theory, growing it from language successful people use into a field of techniques and practices used to influence thoughts, tap into feelings, and change behaviors, both for yourself and for others.

Bandler and Grinder began looking into methods and techniques from various branches of psychotherapy ('talk therapy'). They were particularly interested in gestalt therapy, which is a branch of psychotherapy that focuses on the present life and current needs of the patient, rather than bringing up their past experiences and traumas. It places focus on understanding the context of what a person is going through and the challenges they're facing. Bandler and Grinder continued to grow and form their theory and the practice that accompanied it. They studied the language patterns used by effective therapists and read up on the techniques behind their skill, adding this to their growing database used to create NLP.

Bandler and Grinder titled their first book on neuro linguistic programming *The Structure of Magic*. The main focus of the book was to identify the language patterns of renowned and effective therapists. As they developed the theory of NLP, Bandler and Grinder began to branch out, adding to NLP with parts from the theory of medical or therapeutic hypnotism, especially that of psychiatrist Milton H. Erickson. They included Erickson's techniques for conversational hypnosis in their growing set of principles and techniques that were soon to emerge as neuro-linguistic programming.

Alongside that, they added the theories and structure of Noam Chomsky, the renowned linguist and cognitive scientist who developed transformational grammar, to form a steadfast crossover between psychology and linguistics known as 'NLP'. Since then, many others have tried out the techniques and practices of NLP and have become life-long devotees to the theory. Today, the field of NLP has grown wide and prosperous, with many different people writing, researching, and contributing to the NLP community. One that you are soon to enter, too! With the origin story told, it's now time to move on to...

STARTER TECHNIQUES FOR NLP

As we've seen, neuro linguistic programming is about how we communicate, both with other people and with ourselves. It also analyzes the way we communicate and the effect it has on the way you and your audience behave. Finally, NLP is used to influence people's emotional and behavioral outcomes (the way we feel and act). Beyond that, NLP will also help to increase your self-confidence and self-awareness, as well as greatly enhance your communication skills. It's also an extension of, or next step to, separating the map from the territory and setting the context of the conversation, as we covered back in Chapter 3. Let's go over the main beginner techniques of this fascinating field of study. Soon, you'll be such a wizard with words that nobody will be able to resist your charm nor overcome your conversational prowess.

Build Rapport

If we have good rapport with someone, we have a close and friendly relationship with them. We understand one another's concerns and respect each other's feelings. This allows for the usual social barriers to be lowered, resulting in a smoother flow of thoughts and ideas. This is the type of relationship we have with our family (the ones we're on good terms with) and our close friends. When we're around such people, there's not only a free-flow of conversation, but we also tend to take on the mannerisms and phrasing that we associate with that person or group of people. This is 'rapport', a vital skill for anyone looking to win every argument and piss people off in the right way, and yes, building rapport is indeed a skill that can be learned. You can't fake years, decades even, of memories, but you can activate your audience's feelings of familiarity and aim them toward you. To do this, we use two NLP techniques: Mirroring and matching.

Mirroring and Matching

Although it may not feel like it to some, we humans are very similar in many different ways. The way we move, act, sound, gesture, even think, is determined by the way that those around us move, act, sound, gesture and think. This isn't the case for everyone, just those stuck confusing the map for the territory. You can use this to your advantage by mimicking or mirroring their gestures, posture, facial expressions, sitting position, and even cursing words. By doing this, you can make the other person feel like you are familiar, and they will then start treating you like someone who is from the same 'area' as them.

Begin by observing and make sure not to overdo it or you'll make it obvious that you're trying to copy their body language. Before you begin mirroring in a conversation, begin by observing the way that closer friends mirror one another when chatting. See how often they mirrored each other, how long after the action the mirroring occurred, and whether it was reciprocated by the other side at any time. Once you have observed how and how often people mirror each other, take it out and test it. Try to consciously control your mirroring and matching of your close friends and family. Once you've got the hang of that, test it out with complete strangers.

You can also get very specific with the way that you mirror the other person or match their movements. You can, for example, mirror their blinking speed or match their tone of voice. Mirroring and matching work wonders, all the way up until anger is involved. If someone is downright pissed with you, then mirroring their anger is not going to do you any favors in winning that argument. In fact, it's probably going to get you a black eye at the least. In the case that you find yourself face-to-face with an angry human, remain calm, take a neutral stance, and focus more on logic and argumentation than on emotion or persuasion. That's if they're angry with you. If they're angry with someone or something else, then you can mirror their hand gestures and definitely bank on emotion and persuasion to get the job done.

Get Meta

One of the catchwords of the 21st century, 'meta' means to show awareness of oneself or to be self-referential (refer to yourself in the third-person, for example). This makes getting meta a great addition to separating the map from the territory and for setting the context of the conversation. There are two NLP techniques based on getting meta. They are:

Meta Positioning

Meta positioning means taking the point of view that we just talked about above. Imagine yourself in a position just above and outside of your current one. Claiming this vantage point, what would you see? How would you feel about the current argument point or debate topic if you were removed from the emotional shell that is your body? This is a kind of dissociation technique that allows you to analyze things from a much more logical, less emotional perspective. After you have done that, ask a question based on your meta-positioned thoughts and pose it to your conversation partner or to the group. You could also take the 'position' of your argument partner or a member of the audience and view things from their perspective. Formulate a question based on your meta-positioning and ask it before providing the answer. For example: "You may be wondering X, Y, and Z. Well, you see, A, B, C."

Taking this kind of meta position helps us to gain more insights and see different approaches to a situation. In other words, it helps us to separate our mental map from the territory that is the conversation.

Meta Modeling

Linked to meta positioning is meta modeling. Where the former has to do with taking a third-person viewpoint or a different perspective to a conversation, meta modeling has to do with building a 'model' of yourself or the person you are conversing with. When creating your model of the person, don't focus on taking their position, but rather focus on what you perceive to be the model of them that agrees with your point of view. Then, mind-map out a way to get from A (reality) to B (your model).

Modeling

The next NLP skill to add to your repertoire is modeling. This technique is similar to the meta modeling that we just looked at but is more focused on copying someone else rather than creating a meta-model of them. Since we now all agree that the map is not the territory, why not constantly add to our mental maps? If you see a mannerism or gesture that you like, model it and add it to your repertoire. Doing this is the same as when you hear or read some thought point, opinion, or belief, and you take it on as your own. Most people model others subconsciously. Those that know a thing or two about NLP bring this into the conscious world as they continuously add to and update their mental maps. Let's go through the three phases of modeling.

Phase 1: Observe

The first step to successfully replicating something is to find someone to use as a model. It's preferable to find someone in person, although this isn't always possible. Movies are also a great source to use. John Grinder calls this "finding your genius", in terms of finding someone who is a 'genius' at what you're trying to do. Once you've found this person, imagine what it's like to view things from their point of view. Imagine what they do, how they do it, and why they do it. These three questions cover the behavior, thought processes, and supporting beliefs of your model. Once you understand this, you have all the background info you need to move onto phase 2.

Phase 2: Practice Until You Can Teach It

The best way to know something properly is to teach it. Being a teacher is quite the thing. You have to know everything (or, at least, know how to look like you do), going from beginner, through to advanced, and then back again as you teach what you learned. Take on this mindset, practicing until you can teach what you're trying to learn to someone else with the confidence that you'll seem like a 'teacher' and not some guy doing bad impressions on the street. Remember that rehearsal is a key part of modeling, whichever way we define the word. Model away like you're learning some new dance move, for that's what it is, in the verbal dance we call a conversation.

Six-Step Reframing

The final NLP beginner skill that we're going to look at is the six-step reframe technique. This has to do with rewiring our behaviors through reframing our motives. One of the core NLP presuppositions is that every behavior we have and response we make has an intent. What this means is that our motives, what we believe in, drives our behaviors and how we act. As we grow up, we try out many different attitudes and behaviors, keeping some and discarding others as easily as we would change our style of clothing. But, as we get older, our fashion sense solidifies, as do our beliefs and behaviors. Not so for the NLP initiate though! Let me show you how to use motive to break free from the ruts of habit and complacency.

Identify

The first step of reframing is to identify the specific behavior, gesture, mannerism, or belief that you want to change. Really focus in, analyzing it from all angles and tracking it back to its roots. Make a mind map to visualize the behavioral pattern and identify the specific parts that you want to change. Think about why you want to change it and how it will make your life better once it has changed.

Communicate Your Intent

Once you have identified and analyzed the behavior or response you want to change, the next step is to visualize it and 'communicate' your intent. Close your eyes and consciously try to focus on the unwanted behavior, or alternatively, meditate on your mind map of it. Connect with it and communicate your positive intent, or will, for it to change.

Focus on the Positive

While it's sad to say, many people in this world focus more on the negatives than they do on the positives. This is especially true when it comes to the way they view and talk to themselves, but this is not the way of the person wise to the teachings of neuro-linguistic programming. I'm sure we've all heard a quote like, "What you put out to the universe is what you get," or something along those lines, but what if I told you that this is true; it does happen. Only, it's not the universe that's doing it, but our own brains. Have you heard of the Law of Attraction before? We're not going to get too much into it here, but the basic philosophy of the Law of Attraction is that positive thinking ushers in a positive reality. As such, if you want to make a lasting positive change to a behavior or response, focus on the positive of what the benefits will be once you perfect it, not on the negative of analyzing the unwanted behavior or getting down because of how crappy you are at the new response when first testing it out. Center on the silver lining and watch it soon bloom into full sunshine.

Once you have identified the positives of the change that you're making, use these as the fuel for your intent to make the change. There are few things more powerful in the world than someone driven by a positive intention. If you live by the way of positive intent, you'll seem to brighten up the room just through the presence of your personality. And, if you present yourself this way, no matter how heated or negative the other side of the argument gets, you'll soon become their silver lining, priming them for changing their thoughts or beliefs. It's also a great technique for winning arguments with panache and pissing people off the right way. As Monty Python says: "Always look on the bright side of life!"

Get Creative

Once you have identified the unwanted behavior or response and communicated your positive intent, the next step is to access your creative side and think of all the great functions and uses of your brand-new behavior. One great way to activate your creative brain? Mind map it out! Put your positive intent into words and place it in the central circle. Then, think of all the possibilities this new behavior will have on your performance, how it will help you, and when and where you can use it. Also, list out at least three ways you can start using your intended change straight away. Just through the act of visualizing this new behavior and imagining its multitude of possibilities, you are accessing your creative mind and improving your chances of ingraining the new response in your daily life quickfast.

Evaluate and Create a Link to the Future

A key part of this NLP technique is to evaluate your progress in utilizing the intended change. This evaluation needs to be done with a focus on positive progress, not negative lack of improvement, as well as be carried out as objectively as possible. Emotion doesn't help with this unless it's linked to your positive intent. Linking your present actions to achieving a future goal is known as 'future pacing'. Set some measurable milestones of your progress along the route, evaluate, reflect, and adapt your plan according to your progress. This is how those who know about NLP learn and manage to adopt a new mannerism or gesture as easily as someone learning a new skill in their sport.

Monitor for Knock-On Effects

Once you have practiced and perfected the new behavior or response you were reframing for, the final thing to do is to monitor the ecology of your behavior for any knock-on effects that this newly updated or upgraded response has on the rest of your system. If you change something in a natural environment or computer code, it's going to have knock-on effects throughout the system. It's the same with the human mind and body. So, monitor yourself for changes in your behavior, and if the knock-on effect doesn't sit well with the new you, go back to step 2 and get reframing!

With the six-step reframing technique outlined and defined, we come to the end of this chapter on the basics of neuro-linguistic programming. Master these techniques and you'll start to gain more and more control of your mind, allowing you to separate the map from the territory and set the context of the conversation. In the next chapter, we're going to go a bit more in-depth into an important concept of NLP that we touched on briefly in this chapter: Reframing.

7

IN THROUGH THE OUT DOOR

Reframing, the art of separating the map frame the territory, is a useful and frequently used practice in NLP. Our minds are continuously framing and reframing our representations of reality based on the information coming in and the way we choose to interpret it, both consciously and subconsciously. As we saw when we learned about mind mapping, whenever we think of something, we automatically link related ideas to it and place it in the tangled web of a map that is our understanding of reality.

In this chapter, we're going to outline the magic of reframing before covering three techniques—Content Reframe, Context Reframe, and Outer Framing. Once armed with these techniques, you'll be able to see the bigger picture of how to potentially reframe any discussion, topic, or notion that you choose!

THE MAGIC OF REFRAMING

Whenever we think about something, we always put it into some frame of reference. Without framing what we think, we wouldn't be able to think about things at all. When we frame a thought or idea, we put it into a certain category; defining what it means and associating it to other similar or related thoughts or ideas we've had in the past. We also take into account the frame of reference that is our current surroundings and a multitude of other factors that add up to the average person's view of reality.

At its core, reframing has to do with changing the way we think about something and to begin using a different frame of reference or reference structure. In the previous chapter, we covered the six-step process of how we reframe our own thoughts, but it's also possible to reframe the thoughts of others during a conversation. Even if you manage to do this ever so slightly, you've won. If you can provide your audience with a new frame of reference during a conversation, link it to something they already believe in, and show how it's beneficial for them to see things from this new frame of reference, you're onto a winner.

The Seven Directions of Reframing

If we think of the great reframers of the past century, we're thinking of people like Steve Jobs, Elon Musk, and Oprah Winfrey. These are the pioneers who changed, or at least influenced, the frames of reference of millions of people around the world. Besides being skilled at creating something new in the world, these people are also highly skilled at articulating their ideas, framing a vivid picture of their vision, their dream, that everyone can see, understand, and reframe their own reference point accordingly. Added to this is obviously having the facts and figures, the proof and the passion, to show people the benefit of believing what you've got to say.

In order to begin framing and reframing, you need to take the point of view that nothing has meaning on its own. 'Meaning' is a human construct that determines what and how we think about something. Two people can look at an open field after the rain, with the one framing the picture with the meaning of beauty and nature, and the other framing the scenery as muddy with a chance of cow patties on the unavoidable walk back that is certain to ruin their shoes. A silly example, but one that captures the way that people can look at the same thing and live through the same experience but put different meaning to the different parts depending on how it fits in with their frame of reference.

Knowing this, the trick then becomes to find a way to connect what you've got to say to a previously existing reference point in the mental map of your audience. Let's cover seven directions, or dimensions, of reframing. This theory comes from a book by Dr. Michael Hall and Dr. Bob Bodenhamer titled: *Mind Lines: Lines for Changing Minds* (1997).

- **Deframing**

  Deframing has to do with taking a piece of meaning apart, separating it from its context, and dissecting it through analysis.

- **Reframing**

  As we've covered already, reframing has to do with changing the way you think or act to a new idea or action. It also has to do with reclassifying information.

- **Pre-framing**

Much like foreshadowing in a book or movie, pre-framing is where you set the context or frame of reference before sharing your perspective. An example of this would be to tell a short story at the beginning to set the tone of your point and build the scene in the mind of your audience.

- **Post-framing**

Whereas pre-framing is about establishing a perspective ahead of time, post-framing is about imagining a future perspective looking back on the action or point you're making. This allowed for a fresh viewpoint that can often offer new insights or different meanings.

- **Counter-framing**

This frame happens in the action of a debate or argument, and deals with providing counter arguments, explanations, or examples.

- **Outframing**

Outframing takes "look at the bigger picture" to heart as it deals with trying to get your audience to place a new meaning on something based on the 'grander-scale' frame you've shown them.

- **Metaphorical Framing**

The final reframing direction makes use of the power of story. In metaphorical framing, you turn your argument points and rebuttals into meaningful analogies spiced with powerful metaphors.

Using the seven directions of reframing, you can start to not only reframe the context of your own mind, but also the mental maps of those you talk to. Remember that it's not a "one-size-fits-all" kind of deal, and it's not going to be a one and done either. In fact, I recommend making a mind for each of your arguments and think about what you could say for the seven directions of reframing for each of them. Challenge yourself to consider your viewpoint from every frame of reference and consider how best to utilize that frame to get people to see this from your point of view.

Content Reframe

To put it simply, content reframe is the NLP way of saying, "Always look on the bright side of life," the core of the concept being to put a positive twist on a negative thought, belief, behavior, or event. Another name for this reframing technique is 'meaning reframe', as that's exactly what you're trying to do: Change the meaning of something negative to instead focus on creating a more positive framework based on that event. This can help you to overcome any unwanted emotions you may feel or to come to terms with events outside of your ability to control and overcome them through handling yourself right in these situations.

The meaning we put onto anything is determined by what we choose to focus our attention on. In order to reframe the meaning of a situation, you need to first begin by becoming fully aware of the behavior or response that you want to change. Then, use the six-step reframing process we covered in the previous chapter to create the new and improved content or positive meaning. There is always more than one meaning to be attached to something, so why not choose the one with the most positive intent? This is what reframing, and the entire theory of NLP, is about: Using language, both spoken and internal, to spread positivity and improvement. Questions that fall under content reframing include: "What else could this mean?" and, "In what way could I view this as a positive?"

Believe it or not, a central assumption, or presupposition even, of NLP is that every behavior and response that we have has a positive intention, a purpose. This is true for yourself and for other people, and if you think this isn't true for any of your behaviors or responses, or that they no longer fit with the present version of you, then go through the six-step process and change them.

Context Reframe

While content reframing is better used to change unwanted behaviors or negative thought patterns, context reframing is most useful in dealing with things in the moment or in helping with sensory overload. It does this through changing the way you react to certain contexts and situations. Context, in NLP terms, is the specific setting the conversation occurs in and the situations attached to it. Every meaning we attach to something is context dependent. We wouldn't wear a bikini to a business meeting or a business suit to the beach, after all!

When we talk about context reframe, we're talking about reframing the meaning we attach to something by changing the context we associate with it. This means taking someone's point or meaning and placing it into a different context that undermines its meaning or even makes it seem nonsensical. Context reframing is a great way of showing people how the meaning of something changes when you change its context. To understand the difference between content reframe and context reframe, let's look at some examples. These will also help to show these two NLP techniques in action.

'I am too needy!'

<u>Content Reframe:</u> How can you aim that 'neediness' of yours in a direction that benefits your day-to-day, such as needing to complete your tasks and deadlines.

<u>Context Reframe</u>: Compared to who? You're no drug addict, so you're doing well. Just remember to take everything in moderation, and you'll be A-okay.

'I can't stop procrastinating!'

<u>Content Reframe:</u> When you procrastinate, do some menial activity and turn it into a positive procrastination session. Make a list of activities to do for positive procrastination and, when you find yourself lost in a daydream or death scroll, do one of your positive procrastination activities instead.

<u>Context Reframe:</u> Would you procrastinate with your life? Giving away hour by hour, day by day of your life to the god of procrastination, aka death. If you can't stop procrastinating, you can't stop feeding death your most precious possession: Time.

'I always seem to focus on what could go wrong.'

<u>Content Reframe:</u> Trying to focus your attention on other elements besides yourself is a good start to developing empathy and heightened awareness. Make sure to balance those thoughts on what could go right so that you get the full 360-degree treatment!

<u>Context Reframe:</u> There are many places where this type of attention to detail is critical, such as when building a spaceship or being a detective. You have developed the skill of spotting mistakes easily but should remember this is just one skill in your repertoire, and you have many others to focus on, too.

Outframing

The final of our reframing techniques is called 'outframing', and is greatest for getting rid of, or at least detangling a bit, our limiting beliefs. The idea behind outframing is to take a step back and try to see things from a wider frame of reference. You can even take multiple 'steps back', widening the frame of reference each time. As we mentioned, this technique is great for analyzing your limiting beliefs so that you can begin detangling them from your mind. Limiting beliefs are those that hold us back and stop us from performing at our best or achieving what we could otherwise have accomplished. In the book *The Encyclopedia of Systemic NLP and New Coding,* written by NLP coaches Robert Dilts and Judith DeLozier, this process of changing our limiting beliefs is called 'Belief Outframing'. Dilts and Delozier suggest taking three different frames of reference. They are:

- First position (your point of view).
- Second position (your close friend or mentor; someone who believes in you).
- Third position (an observer able to see all the networks and systems you are a part of, the environments you influence and are influenced by, and the relationships you have within these environments).

Then, apply past, present, and future to each of the above frames to bring the total number of belief outframes to nine. Once you have reflected or meditated on each of these frames of reference for your specific limiting belief, you'll soon find it has much less of a hold on you than before. Combine this with the other NLP techniques we've covered, and you've taken the next few leaps along the path to not only winning every argument and pissing people off the right way, but also for becoming a new and improved version of yourself. In the next chapter, we're going to move on from reframing meaning to looking at meaning itself as we learn the final few NLP tools for you to become a pro context setter and a wizard with words able to change someone's beliefs in the course of one or two conversations.

8

SAY WHAT YOU MEAN, OR IS IT THE OTHER WAY ROUND?

Welcome, my argumentative king or persuasive queen, to the final chapter of our book! It's been excellent having you on board for our learning journey through the world of winning arguments and pissing people off the right way. In this final chapter, we're going to be speaking about meaning, and what the word 'meaning' really means. Know what I mean? We'll be giving it an NLP twist as we look at the link between truth and paradox and learn how to define our purpose in relation to the larger scope of the world we find our meaning from.

The meaning of 'meaning' can only be interpreted in terms of what it does to us. The meaning that we assign to something tends to be very subjective and more than a bit biased, and this is how it naturally needs to be.

What something means to us affects us physiologically, neurologically, and emotionally, but as we have seen, it's possible to change the content and the context of what something means to us, and therefore master meaning rather than letting it master us. Our next step on this path begins with a talk about truths and paradoxes.

OF PARADOX AND TRUTH

A paradox is a statement that at first seems to be contradictory or even absurd, but when further explained or analyzed, can be true. The paradox of meaning or perspective is that we need fiction in order to tell facts. Don't believe me? Let me prove it to be true. When we live through an experience, we do so through our own frame of reference, which is formed by the information our five senses are able to gather and tinted by our thoughts and beliefs. That's when we're living through the experience. Now, fast-forward to you retelling the story to someone else a day, a week, a month, a year, 10 years later. At best, you'll remember the main plot points, and your brain is going to make up the rest from whatever information is left, gluing it all together from whatever else it can find that seems to fit with your representation of reality.

Now, let's look at it from the other side, taking the perspective of the listener to this experience you had. Their ability to understand and comprehend what you're saying has to go through a gauntlet of obstacles. The first one being how skilled the person sharing the experience is at telling a story. The second being the surrounding context of the situation. The third, how well the experience being shared fits in with their own representation of reality. And so, because it's impossible to remember everything factually, and because no-one would listen to you if you did, we need fiction in order to share a factual situation.

Paradoxes and Philosophical Puzzles

What does this mean for you and your journey of winning arguments and pissing people off the right way? Definitely not that you have a free license to just make stuff up. This doesn't work, anyway, because it won't carry the same feeling as something you truly believe in, and it's all about the feels at the end of the day. What it does mean is that you should come to terms with the fact that meaning is largely subjective, and people can only see things through their representation of reality. Knowing this and knowing the argumentation, communication, conversation, and persuasion skills that you do, you are primed for telling the truth through facts intertwined with fiction and storytelling techniques.

The famous Danish physicist and Nobel Prize winner Niels Bohr once said: "The opposite of a true statement is a false statement, but the opposite of a profound truth can be another profound truth." Let's go through a few paradoxes, some of them profound truths while others are fun philosophical puzzles you can use to spice up a conversation.

The Liar

This is an age-old paradox which dates back to ancient Greece, brought to us by a seer named Epimenides. A 'seer' is someone who was supposed to have supernatural insights and to be capable of seeing into the future. Being from Crete, Epimenides once famously said, "All Cretans are liars." This gave rise to the Liar paradox. Let's say someone told you that they were lying. Said it straight out: "I am lying." If what they say is true, then they are lying, which means that what they're saying is false, but if what they told you was false, then they would be lying, which means that what they told you was true. This is a fun paradox puzzle to do with friends who enjoy the more philosophical kinds of conversations.

The Axioms of Communication

The Five Axioms of Communication is a theory created by Austrian American psychologist and psychotherapist Paul Watzlawick and forms a part of his larger theory of misunderstanding. This is based on the paradox of choosing to avoid or ignore metacommunication during a conversation. By 'metacommunication', we mean everything besides speaking. This includes facial expressions, body language, emotions, and so on. Believe it or not, many of the skills and techniques we've covered so far, as simple or obvious as they may seem after reading them, are avoided by many. This led Watzlawick to form the axioms of communication to combat this paradox. They are:

1. It's Impossible to Not Communicate

We are communicating every moment of every day. Either with other people or with ourselves. Even when we watch TV or listen to a podcast, we are communicating with this information. Silence itself is a form of communication and can be less silent than you think in terms of the messages your body is transmitting and the context of your silence.

2. Communication is About More Than the Message

All communication has at least two levels: The content level and the context level. As we covered in the previous chapter when we talked about reframing, content is what you're talking about while context is the situation and relations of the conversation topics to the lives of the speaker and listener. As such, communication is about building relationships.

3. The Communicative Process is the Perfect Feedback Loop

Have you ever found that you could explain an idea you had much better to someone else than you could when just thinking about it yourself? Having a living, breathing soundboard for our ideas is what has escalated humans to be so far at the top of the food chain that we've pretty much separated ourselves from it. This is all because of our ability to communicate. As such, it should be a skill that we all aim to perfect as much as we possibly can, for not only the betterment of ourselves, but the betterment of humankind.

And that is why communication skills and techniques, like all of those covered in this book, are essential for anyone who wants to get anywhere in the world of today. As we have come to learn, it goes a lot deeper than just the words that we say and the way that we say them and is a lot more learnable and able to be developed than previously thought too. With that final thought on paradoxes and truths, and the relationship between them, we come to the end of this chapter and to the end of our journey into the world of winning arguments and pissing people off just right!

CONCLUSION

To the end we have come. What a journey it has been, taking you through the ropes and learning the lengths and breadth of winning arguments, being convincing, and using neuro-linguistic programming to get what you want while still somehow managing to piss people off in a way that makes them love you and believe in you and your ideas the more for it, too. Soon, your prowess with the spoken word and skill in presenting yourself and your argument points will seem like some kind of magic trick to those that converse with you or and debate against you.

Remember that it goes a lot further than the words you say and the way that you say it. You have to learn to read the room, as well as actively listen to your audience. You have to learn how to separate the map from the territory so that you can start reframing every conversation to a context that fits your audience's needs and your desires. It's also vital to mind-map out your argument points so that you have the information, the facts, the figures at the ready to aid you in reframing through content. Finally, take a step back and view the bigger picture because winning an argument or changing someone's mind isn't a one-time shoe-shine type of deal. It's a lifestyle that can help both you and those that you influence to live a better, more fulfilling life, and what could be better than that?

REFERENCES

Ables, K. (2023). *Walk a Mile in My Shoes*. Kim Abeles. https://kimabeles.com/walk-a-mile-in-my-shoes/#:~:text=Walk%20a%20Mile%20in%20My%20Shoes%20is%20a%20variation%20of

Adlam, C. (2015). *A short History of NLP (Neuro-Linguistic Programming)*. Www.linkedin.com. https://www.linkedin.com/pulse/short-history-nlp-neuro-linguistic-programming-chris-adlam/

Alison. (2023). *Effective Learning Strategies in NLP*. Alison.com. https://alison.com/course/effective-learning-strategies-in-neuro-linguistic-programming?utm_source=bing&utm_medium=cpc&utm_campaign=436347240&utm_content=1350202087964114&utm_term=kwd-84388782265337:loc-168&msclkid=4e67e830cae41977c4ea8c0622dce1a3

Aquino, J. (2016). *Persuasion Skills: How to Use the Power of Emotion to Influence Your Audience*. Cool Communicator. https://coolcommunicator.com/persuasion-skills-power-of-emotion/#:~:text=PERSUASION%20SKILLS%3A%20HOW%20TO%20USE%20THE%20POWER%20OF%20EMOTION%20TO%20INFLUENCE%20YOUR%20AUDIENCE

Bechara, A. (2004). The role of emotion in decision-making: Evidence from neurological patients with orbitofrontal damage. *Brain and Cognition, 55*(1), 30–40.

https://doi.org/10.1016/j.bandc.2003.04.001

Bradberry, T. (2022). *Emotionally Intelligent Arguing*. TalentSmartEQ. https://www.talentsmarteq.com/articles/emotionally-intelligent-arguing/#:~:text=Manage%20your%20own%20feelings%20as

Braithwaite, L. (2020). *There's a right way to piss people off*. Www.linkedin.com. https://www.linkedin.com/pulse/theres-right-way-piss-people-off-lisa-braithwaite-ma-she-her-/

Casabianca, S. (2021). *15 Cognitive Distortions to Blame for Your Negative*

Thinking. Psych Central. https://psychcentral.com/lib/cognitive-distortions-negative-thinking

Cherry, K. (2023). *How to Read Body Language and Facial Expressions*. Verywell Mind. https://www.verywellmind.com/understand-body-language-and-facial-expressions-4147228#:~:text=Body%20lan guage%20refers%20to%20the%20nonverbal%20signals%20that

Clarke, J. (2023). *How Gestalt Therapy Works*. Verywell Mind. https://www.verywellmind.com/what-is-gestalt-therapy-4584583#SnippetTab

Clemente, S. (2022). *Paradoxical Communication: 6 Keys to Understanding it*. Exploring Your Mind. https://exploringyourmind.com/paradoxi cal-communication-6-keys-to-understanding-it/

Cuofano, G. (2023). *Neuro-Linguistic Programming In A Nutshell*. Four-WeekMBA. https://fourweekmba.com/neuro-linguistic-program ming/#:~:text=Neuro%2DLinguistic%20Programming%20In% 20A%20Nutshell

Disabilitynorm. (2020). *(P7): The Map is Never the Territory*. Changes-trategy.net. https://changestrategy.net/2020/08/24/p7-the-map-is-never-the-territory/#:~:text=Confusing%20the%20map%20for% 20the%20territory%20is%20a

Duigan, B. (2023). *8 Philosophical Puzzles and Paradoxes*. Encyclopedia Britannica. https://www.britannica.com/list/8-philosophical-puzzles-and-paradoxes

Dunlop, M. (2014). *The Key Skills of NLP in a Nutshell*. Www.linkedin.-com. https://www.linkedin.com/pulse/20141113173650-70881305-the-key-skills-of-nlp-in-a-nutshell/

Elston, T. (2019). *Eye Patterns & NLP Coaching*. NLP World. https://www.nlpworld.co.uk/nlp-coaching-eye-patterns/#:~:text= Common%20%28but%20not%20universal%29%20Western%20lay out%20of%20eye

Engaged HR. (2016). *Communication: The Importance of Context*. Engaged HR. https://engagedhr.com/the-importance-of-context/#: ~:text=Communication%3A%20The%20Importance%20of% 20Context

Ferriss, T. (2009). *The Benefits of Pissing People Off*. The Blog of Author

Tim Ferriss. https://tim.blog/2009/11/25/the-benefits-of-pissing-people-off/#:~:text=BY%20TIM%20FERRISS-

Goldhill, O. (2015). *Keep losing arguments? A psychologist explains why emotions are more persuasive than logic.* Quartz. https://qz.com/521628/keep-losing-arguments-a-psychologist-explains-why-emotions-are-more-persuasive-than-logic#:~:text=Keep%20losing%20arguments%3F%20A%20psychologist%20explains%20why%20emotions%20are%20more%20persuasive%20than%20logic

Goman, C. K. (2019). *Body Language of Listeners.* Global Listening Centre. https://www.globallisteningcentre.org/body-language-of-listeners/

Hall, M. (2010). *The Magic You Can Perform With Reframing.* Neuro-Semantics. https://www.neurosemantics.com/the-magic-you-can-perform-with-reframing/#:~:text=The%20Magic%20You%20Can%20Perform%20With%20Reframing

Hypno Society. (2019). *9 Best NLP Techniques that will Help Change You Realize your Potential.* HypnoSociety.com. https://hypnosociety.com/nlp-techniques/

Landsiedl. (2023). *Six-Step Reframing.* Www.landsiedel.com. https://www.landsiedel.com/en/nlp-library/six-step-reframing.html#:~:text=Six-Step%20Reframing%20-%20Steps%201%20Identify%20the%20pattern

Life Enrich. (2023). *NLP Reframing - Content Reframe and Context Reframe.* NLP Practitioner Training | Hypnotherapy | Coaching | Counselling - Life Enrich. https://www.life-enrich.com/en/online-learning/nlp-reframing.html

Mandriota, M. (2021). *What Is NLP?* Psych Central. https://psychcentral.com/health/neurolinguistic-programming-nlp

NLP Education World. (2020). *How to Build a Strong Rapport using NLP Mirroring And Matching Techniques.* NLP Education World. https://nlpeducationworld.com/how-to-build-a-strong-rapport-using-nlp-mirroring-and-matching-techniques/#:~:text=If%20you%20want%20to%20build%20a%20strong%20rapport

NLP Mastery. (2015). *What does context reframing mean?* Anilthomasnlp.com. https://www.anilthomasnlp.com/faq-nlp/

what-does-context-reframing-mean%3F#:~:text=Context%20Fram
ing%20means%20giving%20another%20meaning%20to%20a

NLP Mentor. (2011a). *Eye Body Language - Knowing What People are Thinking.* NLP Mentor. https://nlp-mentor.com/eye-body-language/

NLP Mentor. (2011b). *NLP Modeling, finding the structure of excellence.* NLP Mentor. https://nlp-mentor.com/nlp-modeling/

NLP Mentor. (2011c). *Representational Systems.* NLP Mentor. https://nlp-mentor.com/representational-systems/

NLP Mentor. (2011d). *The Map is not the Territory.* NLP Mentor. https://nlp-mentor.com/map-is-not-the-territory/#:~:text=What%20is%20NLP

NLP Mentor. (2011e, May 6). *The Six Step Reframe Technique.* NLP Mentor. https://nlp-mentor.com/six-step-reframe/

NLP Mentor. (2015). *Neuro Linguistic Programming - Changing Behavior and Thinking.* NLP Mentor. https://nlp-mentor.com/neuro-linguistic-programming/

NLP World. (2021). *NLP Context | NLP World - Glossary.* NLP World. https://www.nlpworld.co.uk/nlp-glossary/c/context-reframe/

Nordquist, R. (2018). *What Does Argumentation Mean?* ThoughtCo. https://www.thoughtco.com/what-is-argumentation-1689133

Northeastern Global News. (2017). *"If you can't explain it to a 6-year-old, you don't understand it yourself."* News @ Northeastern. https://news.northeastern.edu/2017/04/13/if-you-cant-explain-it-to-a-6-year-old-you-dont-understand-it-yourself/#:~:text=%E2%80%9CIf%20you%20can

Psychology Today. (2019). *Body Language.* Psychology Today. https://www.psychologytoday.com/us/basics/body-language

Rational Wiki. (2014). *Logical fallacy .* Rationalwiki.org. https://rationalwiki.org/wiki/Logical_fallacy

Rational Wiki. (2023). *Mistaking the map for the territory.* RationalWiki. https://rationalwiki.org/wiki/Mistaking_the_map_for_the_territory#:~:text=Mistaking%20the%20map%20for%20the%20territory

Rolheiser, R. (1998). *Truth Is Found In Paradox.* Ronrolheiser.com.

https://ronrolheiser.com/truth-is-found-in-paradox/#.
ZEEg2PxBxD-

Ryan, R. (2021). *NLP in a Nutshell*. Rebekah Ryan. https://www.
rebekahryan.com/blog/nlp-in-a-nutshell

Science of People. (2023). *Reading Body Language 101*. Science of People.
https://www.scienceofpeople.com/body-language/body-language-
101/

Smith, A. (2016). *Outframing - a practical NLP process for loosening
limiting beliefs*. Practical NLP. https://nlppod.com/outframing/#:~:
text=Outframing%3A%20A%20Process%20For%20Loosening%
20Limiting%20Beliefs

Van Edwards, V. (2021). *5 Powerful Reasons Why Body Language is Important*. Science of People. https://www.scienceofpeople.com/body-
language-important/

Wingfield, D. (2022a). *NLP Reframing: A Practical Guide to Content
Reframe*. Www.lifecoachhub.com. https://www.lifecoachhub.com/
coaching-articles/nlp-reframing-a-practical-guide-to-content-
reframe-from-an-nlp-coach/120

Wingfield, D. (2022b). *NLP Reframing: A Practical Guide to Content
Reframe (from an NLP coach)*. Www.lifecoachhub.com. https://www.
lifecoachhub.com/coaching-articles/nlp-reframing-a-practical-
guide-to-content-reframe-from-an-nlp-coach/120